Arrivals & Departures

THE SHEARSMAN CHAPBOOK SERIES, 2014

Patricia Debney *Gestation*
juli Jana *ra-t*
Martyn Crucefix *The Time We Turned*
Anthony Rudolf *Go into the Question*
Robert Vas Dias *Arrivals and Departures*

Arrivals & Departures

Prose Poems

Robert Vas Dias

Shearsman Books

First published in the United Kingdom in 2014 by
Shearsman Books
50 Westons Hill Drive
Emersons Green
BRISTOL
BS16 7DF

Shearsman Books Ltd Registered Office
30–31 St. James Place, Mangotsfield, Bristol BS16 9JB
(this address not for correspondence)

www.shearsman.com

ISBN 978-1-84861-365-2

Acknowledgements
Thanks are due to the editors of the following, in which many of these
prose poems were first published, some in earlier versions: *Clang: Prose
Poems, Envoi, Five: Oasis Series 75, The London Magazine, Poetry Salzburg
Review, Poetry Wales, Tears in the Fence*. 'Do Angels Eat,' 'Meditation on a
Return Ticket,' 'Petoskey Stone,' and 'Woodpigeons' appeared in my book
Still · Life and Other Poems of Art and Artifice (Shearsman), and 'August
2011' and 'Life of Bones' appeared in different form in my chapbook
London Cityscape Sijo and Other Poems (Perdika).

Cover image:
Arrivals & Departures, by Julia Farrer,
watercolour & gouache, 2014.
Copyright © Julia Farrer, 2014.

Contents

Rubber Bands	7
Woodpigeons	8
The Shirt	9
Meditation on a Return Ticket	10
Der Blaue Reiter	11
Cannoli	12
Acrobat	13
Cheesed	14
Deadheading the Petunias	15
Road Kill	16
She Knows Where She Stands	17
Do Angels Eat?	18
Numbers	20
The Stymie	21
Love's Pity	22
The Cabinet of Husbands	23
The Last Apple in Leonia	24
Petoskey Stone	25
Eppur si muove	26
Sailor	27
Desert Prose Poems	28
The Thing About Tables	30
Life of Bones	31
August 2011	32
Le vide papier que la blancheur défend	33
Names & Addresses	34

Rubber Bands

Knowing postmen leave me red rubber bands in elastic London streets that change names after short stretches, twist first one way and then the other, coned off by a contraflow of my accustomed ways. Hieroglyphs of curly ellipses, intaglios of ovals, calligraphies of circles and circles within circles, squashed organic writing composed on strange byways, misshapen integers of a strange numerology, compel me to tease the meaning of their anthropological codes. But the red-banded bundles the postman brings me contain little but importunities, attempting to tempt me with new scams, impossible odds, bogus delights: no mysteries in the ephemera that are supposed to change my life.

Woodpigeons

I spent my whole self searching
love which I thought was you

it was mine so briefly
and I never knew it, or you went
                    — Frank O'Hara, 'Poem'

She arrived with the woodpigeons. That is to say, she arrived and they left. Not that she had anything obviously to do with it. Of course she did. She kept on arriving and then she left. They appeared constantly to be fleeing the roost at her, at his, at anyone's approach, though clearly they had to have returned in order to flee again. He never saw them return but they always fled. She came to stay with him and then she went. They – or more usually one of them – would explode out of the treetops with a clatter of wings against foliage that sounded like falling buckshot, and hurl themselves down to the field below the house, where they alighted on the rock walls. They waited, longer than he was prepared to stare at them, or they flew further away. He had to assume their return, never count on it. By saying hello to her was he not already beginning to say goodbye? Her eyes were flecked with green, the same glossy green as on the necks of woodpigeons. They could be heard from afar cooing in the trees. They were there, somewhere, part of an elemental landscape of love and loss. Their departure was sudden, loud, a flight of hysterical panic. She was of a quiet nature, discreet, but she had a flighty disposition. Even when he took them for granted, they all at once insinuated themselves by making a hyper-dramatic and, he thought, totally uncalled-for statement by ostentatiously going away and not returning for an indefinite time which was, for all practical purposes, forever.

The Shirt

When they kissed for the last time and he saw her go through the doors to security, turn once, wave, and disappear from sight, he retraced his steps back to his car in the airport parking lot. As he opened the car door, a faint whiff of her perfume was released which, however, dissipated almost immediately. He drove back down the motorway up which they had travelled not an hour ago, completing the other half of the roundabout the first half of which they had traversed earlier. When he got home he went to the kitchen where the remainder of their breakfast coffee was still hot in the coffee-maker, and poured himself a cup. He went to bed early that evening. Undressing, he pulled his shirt over his head: again the hint of her perfume. As he lay down in the same slight depression their bodies had made he noticed a smudge of dried semen on the bottom sheet of the bed from which they had arisen early that morning, the day's travelling ahead of them.

Meditation on a Return Ticket

> I pick up my life
> and take it away
> on a one-way ticket
> — Langston Hughes

I have a return ticket I will never use because East Midlands Trains made me an offer: it was cheaper to buy a return than to pay for just one way. The offer was that I could go somewhere and come back for less than it took to get there. We're talking money, but time, as they say, is money, and so is space: I could go as far again as the distance I covered in the first place. By standing there I'd have gone twice as far, gained more than I lost, arrived before I left, wishes become actualities. In fact there would be nothing to be imagined, no anticipation or fulfilment, no pleasure, no sorrow, all feeling already felt. It would be like being in a railway coach going forever backward into a dark tunnel leading into the terminus.

Langston was getting out of an impossible situation, an impossible South, starting over. If the offer were available would he have bought the return ticket just to fool them into believing he'd return? I think not. If I took them up on their offer I'd be back where I started, as though I'd never set out full of anticipation at the intimate conversation I'd have with you, as though, after our meeting, I had not been changed forever. I did have the impression the season had changed, it was warmer, but perhaps this was a subtle touch by the rail company, the heating system stuck on 'full', windows jammed, aisles full of passengers sweating out the second leg of a return trip. I would have saved money but have to admit that I fell for their marketing ploy, that all trips were round-trips ending where they began, seamless, purposeless except for the fact of travelling up and down fulfilling some marketing manager's hyped-up scheme of a day out on the rails, and not a journey that goes somewhere and ends somewhere else so you can tell someone you have left, you have arrived.

Der Blaue Reiter

After Kandinsky, 'Zwei Reiter vor Rot,' 1911, woodcut.

Against a sanguine sky the wind scythes leaves off the tree. Your horse, caparisoned in blue, rears in a kind of capriole, prancing and neighing in exhilaration at carrying his blue rider in the wind that sculpts you. I love the way you carry yourself in stormy weather. You are balanced in blue exuberance. We're heading mostly towards the west. Or is it the east? Hard to tell when the whole sky's incarnadine. There's nothing static about our ride, up and down, side to side, the view far and near, colours always changing. In the distance is the mystical city, blue in horizon's blur. When the scene darkens I'll call a halt and we'll bed down for the night. In our sleep everything and nothing makes sense. You tell me your dreams are colourful, that you don't know where they come from, those inexplicable images, as sharply etched in your mind as we are, always riding.

Cannoli

On a hot and humid summer's day languorous Anna-Beth and I thrash through the crowded streets of Little Italy, our clothes stickily clinging. I slip my arm around her waist and she leans into me as we proceed coupled in a dance-like embrace in the mid-day heat. It begins to rain and without umbrellas we are getting wet and sweaty, her fragrance intoxicating me, so we pop in to a nearby pasticceria where we have an espresso, and Anna-Beth fancies a cannoli, which she picks up with her delicate fingers, gently chewing through the hard pastry until the creamy filling oozes from the corners of her mouth.

Acrobat

He is smitten with a young woman who plays the acrobat in a TV series called *The Acrobat*, though he's seen her only on the screen. She has a supple and well-proportioned body and is not particularly beautiful. She isn't even beautiful, mock his friends. All right, he says, but she's a trained *traceuse* of Parkour. What's that? they ask. It's a very demanding gymnastic sport, he explains, you overcome urban obstacles by vaulting, rolling, running, climbing, and jumping. So they employ a look-alike gymnast, they say. No, he says, she does everything herself, she's amazing. In one episode she crosses the highwire between towers of a suspension bridge. Of course, they tell him, since you can't see her face from that distance, the director uses a stuntwoman for the scene. No, he says, I'm certain she does it herself, she's an acrobat. Wake up, they say, she's an actor playing an acrobat, she's not an acrobat in real life. Don't tell me she isn't really an acrobat, he says, she's a *traceuse*, she leaps between the roofs of high buildings. That's obviously a double, they say, they wouldn't risk her falling. He knows what he sees, she's authentic, she's real, they can't imagine the extraordinary positions she could achieve with the éclat of an acrobat.

Cheesed

She bought the sheep cheese thinking it was goat because she knew he detested goat, in fact he got ill just thinking about it. Not that she wanted him to get ill, just not get her tasty goat. He liked sheep cheese as much as he hated goat. Now he would eat the sheep cheese, she knew he would. She wanted the sheep for herself. She wanted their animals, the cats, but they always jumped into his lap, not hers. Sometimes he had two in his lap at a time while she had none. The dogs followed him everywhere, not her. The koi carp in the rock pool gulped to the surface and mouthed their bubbly greetings at his approach, the budgies chirped for him, the mynah bird talked to him, not her. He talked to the horses in the paddock and they neighed and cantered up and nuzzled him. They kept no goats and no sheep, though she would have liked to. He proposed getting a baby conger eel which would thrive on the koi and gradually take over.

Deadheading the Petunias

His darling sent him in the garden to deadhead the petunias but he mistook the limp, budding flowerets for dying ones and twisted them off. You've ruined my petunias, she wailed. Don't be upset, we've still got the weigela. It's not the same, she cried. We've still got the fuchsia. It's not the same, she sobbed. We still have the lobelia, hibiscus, morning glory, wisteria, agapanthus, trachelospermum jasminoides, honeysuckle, grape vine, Japanese maple, pieris forest flame, hydrangea, camellia, geranium, agave, anemone, hellebore. And you have me. Go fuck yourself, she complained.

Road Kill

The restaurant reverberated with noisy conviviality and piped music, and there were eight of us at the table, so when I leaned over to hear the young woman opposite telling a story, I singed my eyebrows on the table-top candle. She and her husband had been driving down a country road when they ran over something. Stop, stop! she cried out, we can pick it up and cook it for dinner. I don't want to eat hedgehog, he said. It wasn't a hedgehog, it was a hare or large rabbit, she retorted. I'm not stopping, he said. But I can make a smashing casserole, she said. I'm not stopping, he said. By this time they had gone a half-mile down the road, arguing all the way. I was so cross that when we got home I refused to prepare supper and slept on the sofa, she said, laughing. How were we meant to respond to this little tale? Was it to display her readiness to spot a chance to save money – they were hard-up university students – and her intrepid resourcefulness, or her husband's squeamishness about eating road kill and his refusal to be bothered? Was her anger of the moment only, or did she feel that their lives together had taken a significant change of direction? Did her withdrawal of conjugal rights foreshadow a split? Would it be an unhappy separation, a messy divorce? Would their child, assuming they had one, be handed back and forth between them, and would he or she grow up to be severely emotionally damaged? Would she go on to do voluntary work in Africa? Would he go back to his mother's cooking? My eyebrows smelt like smoke from a barbecue.

She Knows Where She Stands

She's about to step onto the down escalator but can't make the move. She says she is gravitationally insecure. It's her turn to go but how will she hang on? Hang on? Hang on. Hang . on . The gravitational pull is weak. Attraction is equal and opposite to repulsion. Without gravitational security nothing is certain, nothing can be planned, least of all direction. She will drift away, a balloon without ballast, without moorings. I've had enough of going up and down, leaving at one end and arriving at another. How tired I am of departures and arrivals, hellos and goodbyes, the turning of leaves, the migrations of birds. Where is the end? Everybody expects her to make a move but she prefers to stay put especially if the ground under her feet moves. Did the earth move for you, is for her not a question to raise an enigmatic giggle but the flight response. I will flee anything that conveys me to another land. Level. The level land I find myself on is the one I can stand. Stand up on. Stand on. Don't expect me to live down, or up to, anything. I will fall at my own rate. Don't push.

Do Angels Eat?

After Albrecht Dürer, Melencolia, 1514, engraving

I come down in the morning after a stormy, sleepless night and here's this angel flopped in my garden like García Márquez's old angel with enormous wings but this angel is female, she's not old and she's sitting on the little plinth I was going to put a potted plant on, she's sitting there with a hang-dog look, not dejected really, more of a faraway, contemplative expression as if deep in thought. She doesn't look very happy but maybe happiness has nothing to do with it, maybe yearning, nostalgia, regret, an angelic anguish, she's just down, she's certainly down, ha ha, but I don't feel like laughing. I ask her if she'd like a cup of tea, would you like a cup of tea? I feel like an idiot, how would you feel asking an angel if she'd like a cup of tea, do angels eat? It's said they like manna but I haven't got any, don't even know what it is, have no idea where to buy it. Her wings seem too heavy for her, they're certainly large, their tips are trailing on the ground. She ignores me, she sits there looking rather miserable, how would you look if your wings suddenly got too heavy and you had to make a forced landing in a tiny town garden? She has that blowsy, windblown look. I say, can I help you? – the kind of question you'd ask an intruder so as not to alarm him, not, what the hell are you doing here, and then the bar comes out, the lunge. She acts as if she doesn't hear me, she's somewhere else, far away, she's inside her head, she includes me out. I'm not part of her world, angels don't run in the family. Can I help you, I ask again, gently. Please say something I say, trying not to sound testy. It's as if I'm speaking another language entirely, no, as if I haven't spoken at all. What am I to do? Call the police? The council? How can they help? Take her away? Where? Where does she belong? She doesn't belong to me, does she. She just happens to be in my garden, sitting there dejectedly, well, subdued, compelled by something irreconcilable, overcome by something. Is she sorrowing for our suffering? Maybe she's working out the alchemy of probabilities. I know: she's trying to figure how to fly out. It seems an impossibility, she's like a swan in a very small pond, not enough run for lift-off. She's bound to stay here forever, until… do angels ever die? What will I do with her? If she's here day and night how will I cope? Why has she disturbed my life? How do I reconcile myself to her not answering, not speaking, ignoring me, how do I accept her perched upon the little plinth as though she's perched upon my soul?

Numbers

His appointment is at 13.45. He doesn't want to be late yet he doesn't want to be on time. He has to be there, of course, naturally, absolutely, but he doesn't want to be. Perhaps he doesn't need to. On the other hand, the appointment has been made. It will be unpleasant, of course, naturally, but absolutely necessary of course. Not pleasant. He takes a ticket from the dispensing machine, waits with others waiting, others whose numbers are lower than his, waiting. His number is 68, the number on the board 51. I should have been earlier, he thinks. Number 52 flashes up on the board. He's brought his newspaper and a book, Poe's stories. To take his mind off. An hour at least, he thinks. He begins with Poe: *The thousand injuries of Fortunato I had borne as I best could; but when he ventured upon insult, I vowed revenge. You, who so well know the nature of my soul, will not suppose, however, that I gave utterance to a threat.* Down into the damp catacombs under the city. *You are a man to be missed.* He breathes heavily. The board reads 70. Where have the numbers gone? Time gone? I've missed my number, he explains to the receptionist, easily done when lost in a story, doesn't she agree? Numbers missed. *An excellent jest.* She is adamant he take another ticket, wait his turn like the others waiting, patiently waiting. Not fair. Fair is lost. Clutching number 81, he gets a paper cup of water from the water-cooler and sits down. *To the buried that repose around us. And I to your long life.* His newspaper reports the collapse of banks, the collapse of markets, the collapse of nations. The board reads 83. He jumps up, again appeals to the receptionist. Show me your ticket. His clammy hands have blurred the number into a calligraphic smear. I can't have you jump the queue without a valid ticket, it wouldn't be fair. It's now 16.15, they'll be leaving before your new number comes up, you'll have to come in on the same day next week. *For the love of God. Yes, for the love of God.* Lost is fair. *Let us be gone.*

The Stymie

I can't find my pen and pencil case, she wails, it's got my best, my one-and-only pen. Then she misplaces her watch, and her Freedom Pass goes missing. Next to disappear is her notebook, and her address book along with it. The Yak-Trax are not where they were last seen, and neither is her favourite pashmina. Next to go are her keys, and then her wallet with all her credit cards and some money, disappeared into thin air. Nothing, nothing is where it's supposed to be, or where it was last seen, or where she thought she remembered putting it. All gone, gone into the interstices, the walls of the house closing in.

Love's Pity

They scratched their linked initials on me,

F da R – P M

locked me onto the railings of the Ponte Vecchio and tossed the key into the Arno. The point was to clinch their undying love forever, but it didn't last, did it. Does it ever. Look at it this way: a lock's supposed to keep you or your effects safe, or safer, or give you the illusion you're safe, or convince you you're doing something about keeping safe in an uncertain world, but nothing's ultimately secure, is it. If somebody's intent on breaking or entering, they will. They'll use a hacksaw, they'll hack, these days hack into everything known about you. How secure is undying love? Let's face it, love led those two to a common death at the hands of Francesca's husband who caught them at it in her bedroom. OK, let's admit that in a sense their love survived when you consider it was celebrated, if that's the word, by the poet seven hundred years ago. His poem will probably last longer than I will, hanging here corroding and decomposing as they undoubtedly are, or were. The city fathers, sick and tired of having to cut away all those copycats' love tokens because, they say, they 'disfigure' the Ponte, forbade anyone, in love or not, from attaching locks to the railings. As if an ordinance is going to stop lovesick couples flaunting their faith in their undying love. Fat chance. Those two were condemned to hell where the poet met them and heard their story, *so that because of pity / I fainted, as if I had met my death.** It'll take more than that to shake me, I can tell you, bolt cutters for instance.

* *sì che di pietade / io venni men così com' io morisse.*

The Cabinet of Husbands

You would have to say the cabinet was in need of restoration. It was an antique – 175 years old – and was getting shabby, but she was not one for restoring it. She was not one for restoring anything, except perhaps husbands. He was her fifth, older than her by fifteen years. All her husbands had been older than her, they had a certain patina. She bought antiques only when she was certain about their genuineness. Her husbands had been genuine though they had not worn as well as her antiques. She was fastidious about retaining the patina which she took great care not to darken or feed with linseed oil, instead treating the finish with a dab of beeswax now and then. She liked the way they grew more rickety with time, it made her love them the more. Inside the cabinet she kept framed photographs of her previous husbands. The cabinet's drop-down lid was held by metal rods that lowered it to form a writing desk. A day came when she attempted to open the lid but it refused to budge. She knew what was wrong – the husbands had jammed against one or another of the rods – but she had always managed to coax it open. She tried again, careful not to use too much force, and failed. She resisted the urge to call her husband, who was upstairs and who was lame. She picked up a knife and carefully inserted it in the narrow gap between the lid and the frame and tried to prise one of the husbands away from the rod. She tried three times before her frustration finally caused her to call her husband and explain the problem. He limped downstairs, went over to the cabinet without a word, pulled gently but firmly on the door handle, and opened the lid. As he turned to go back upstairs, she shrieked, so what's the difference, why you and not me? Again without a word, he unzipped his trousers and took out his penis. Then he went upstairs. His framed photograph resides in the cabinet.

The Last Apple in Leonia

Small yellow planet trembling in the field of a telescope focused on the ultimate and wobbly sphere, the last apple in Leonia dangles within a thicket of the firmament, apex of a constellation's branching. What we're seeing is a pre-historic glimmer, the light which sourced the last apple in Leonia no longer with us. A globe of energy is about to hatch: as we blink and shift our lenses, its skin is pecked away and life slips out. Not of this world, the last apple in Leonia is a theorem which has yet to be proved, but somewhere in the garden universe a green globe brims secretly, awaiting the feathered astronomers.

Petoskey Stone

This is a speckled fishback world rippling on the sandy lake-bottom near the shore, glistening when I lift it out. Cold and smooth, it contains many small universes within its fossilized egg-shape – polygonal cells, the smaller wedged between the larger, cell edges serrated like sea shells but water-polished and each with a frozen, dark nucleus. Edges, spots, the small universes fade from the heat of my hand, become a speckled dusty grey. I try caressing it to life-semblance, this egg of lifeless molluscs and cold geometries which has emerged from water, motionless in warmth, never to be alive where it lives in my house between seas.

Eppur si muove

In this city I'm on the move, in fact all moves in this as in every city: schoolgirls in the *campo* jump under the skipping-rope twirled by two mothers revolving their arms in wide arcs, motor launches throb through canals creating wave-wakes lapping against the green seaweeded canal sides, in the *Canale della Giudecca* terns toss on churning waters cleaved by swift-slicing, low-in-the-water *vaporetti* loaded with passengers, embarkation docks on their pontoons lurch in the swell, backpacked tourists shove into narrow *calli*, a gondolier swivels his oar in the water for slow forward motion, gulls swerve and scoop titbits flung by diners under awnings on the *fondamenta*, the rising tide curls over the stone pavement wetting the diners' shoes, cargo scows crunch and thump against stanchions, an obscenely huge cruise ship floats bizarrely above the rooftops. While I'm sauntering across the *ponte* and through the *sottopórtego*, turning my head this way and that, the city sinks quietly into the lagoon to be submerged into eventual immobility.

Sailor

The little sailboat enters the narrow tidal channel, tide low, rocks on either side, rocks to starboard! I yell to the helmsman: visions of being staved in, holed, no stanchions to loop the painter to, water rising to the gunwales, deck slipping out from under me, fight to breathe, waste, the waste, my life before me now after me, swift gull-swerve to snatch it from me, lifted up, bones dropped on the shingle, dry bones left to whiten, jetsam, to be picked up by boys or archaeologists and museumed, idly gazed at by squadrons of schoolchildren herded by frazzled teachers, teachers of my life dressed in feathers.

Desert Prose Poems

After Victor Pasmore, 'Idea for Desert Sand' 1992

1. How to cross the Mojave Desert, Barstow to Needles, on US40 in a car without aircon during the summer daytime

with a minimum of delay because the cat in the back is starting to pant, lookit that cat, the gas-station lady says, lest you cool him down that cat'll surely ex-pire, you got a ice chest back there, you got towels? Lay them towels on the ice and put the cat on the towels, then wet a coupla towels, hang em over your back winders an roll em up, here, lemme show yuh. The towels hang down the inside of the back windows and as we pick up speed the air blows through the car, hits the wet towels and cools the car, the cat. Keep the cat cool and you'll stay alive.

2. Watch where you place your sleeping bag in the desert

A hollow isn't a good idea because you might disturb a rattler, or worse, a coral snake – the deadliest. Choose a flat place, no gopher holes, and don't worry about the coyotes, they'll howl around you for what seems all night, but in the morning when you awake and slither out of the bag, you'll notice coyote tracks not a foot from your sleeping head. This is called coyote stealth reconnaissance.

3. The best time in the desert

is night, the air sharp, the sky so densely black the stars seem to swirl in swathes of light around you and the whole world, and the smell, the smell! the delicious, dry, sweet pungency of sage mixed with acrid dust the dew has settled into the ground and softened to the smell of honey.

4. The second best time in the desert

well, maybe the first, is just before dawn in the northern Sahara, south of Aswan. The bus stops in the middle of nowhere and you get out and walk straight into the desert darkness about a half-mile to watch needles of sun pierce sky fabric, and what follows: dawn pinking the sky, then chink of sun-disk. Praise be Horus-Re, you now have a new day. Don't take snaps.

5. Desert contours

Of course contours of dunes remind you of women's, their hips, waists, breasts, abdomens, round of buttock dunes, an inevitable connection beloved of photographers and lovers of art, but watch it, they shift with the winds, entice you ever further in pursuit of the perfect one you've been searching for all your life, a landscape to lose yourself in, parched, hopeless.

The Thing About Tables

My table, my city containing multitudes, my theatre of beings that act out their desires, wishes, demands. One will attract others, or not: they come together or they hate each other and attempt to bury each other, they hide from me so I end up resenting them. Somebody is directing this scenario and it isn't me. I'm supposed to control them but they control me. They follow their own or a metaphysical script. So much of what they say sounds to me like an egotistical plea to be noticed and made much of. Caress me! croaks a talismanic stone. Sort me out! beg those that yearn to be put in their place. Squeeze me! breathes one whose body, previously squeezed, has a very slender waist. Lay me down somewhere comfortable, implores another. Look at me, one says, do you remember when and how I came to you? Do you know why you keep me, why you are attracted to me, because you are, you know. Do you see how useful I am to you, or do you have me because I'm useless but good-looking? You cannot live without me, can you? You are tied to me as I am to you. Our existence together is a symbiosis based on love and necessity. You can't cast me aside. While you may not always acknowledge me, I am always there for you, I am faithful and usually obedient. I'm not perfect, none of us is, but I'm the best you've got and don't you forget it.

Life of Bones

> It is a hard life,
> with bones under you.
> — Diane Wakoski, 'The Helms Bakery Man'

It's a forgiving life with bones under you you're not conscious of, backbone erect, legs swinging on the walk without pain. Bones feel hard but aren't, they're tender, bruise, throb, need cushioning by disc, meniscus, cartilage, to stop them from wearing you down. It's the pain wears you away with each breath when ribs creak and knees won't flex in the dance.

A life with bones is deceptively hard but not as hard as dry bones unclothed when flesh is not upon them, and the marrow in its narrow channels leaches out, makes not blood nor poetry but leaves the hollows for others to breathe their songs into, dry bones to bang the drum.

August 2011

We drink the wine: back to the kitchen, glasses on the tray, they sway and shatter to the floor, dregs on the carpet. A glass gives shape to what's in it. I've done away with wine-shape in the glasses. No longer life-giving, it is a stain on the carpet, the ground. A man shapes the blood within him. What shape there was, is now dregs on the ground. The dregs, the running dogs, the rats, the traitors. On the ground, beneath our feet, we trample on them. We shall find other glasses, *the tree of liberty must be refreshed from time to time*, guilt no need, *with the blood of patriots & tyrants*. The shape of breakage. The waving of flags.

The quotation in italics is by Thomas Jefferson, in a letter to William Smith, Paris, November 13, 1787.

Le vide papier que la blancheur défend

Hand and arm at the ready, concentrate the brain, don't think of sex, death, or taxes, face the White Tyranny, infiltrate the field – the White's shield – order your Black outriders, besiege White's defence, relay necessary messages, heed the commanding voice, don't surrender to thought's control.

Names & Addresses

i.m. Ian Robinson 1934-2004

The other day when I lifted the phone to ask you for an address and phone number of course you weren't there were you you'd died and I couldn't just ring you up could I. It'd been the most natural thing to lift the phone for I don't know how many years decades so it was an ordinary thing just lift the phone and ask for the phone number you'll know or if you don't you'll give me the name of someone who does they'll know, you'd say and I'd ring them and sure enough they knew. Or you'd ring me hello do you have Martin W's number I've lost it I put it on a piece of paper and can't find it I know I have it somewhere I used to have it I know I did I distinctly remember having it but now I don't.

The other day, you'll get a kick out of this, we were going down to West Sussex to visit friends and before we left I put my address book on the roof of the car while we loaded the rest of our things and when we reached East Grinstead I wanted to check the address and then with that awful feeling you get when suddenly the thought enters your head that maybe just maybe but no I couldn't but yes after scrambling around in the car I could and as a matter of fact I did. I didn't allow my misfortune to spoil our visit honestly I didn't I had a very good time you'll be glad to know but on the drive home became more and more morose and when we arrived walked around the square and down Canonbury Road in the darkness with a torch dodging traffic searching for my address book on the road but no luck then checked the letterbox but no one had found it and dropped it in but damned if there wasn't a message on the answerphone from a "Richard" saying I was cycling through Canonbury Square and spotted your address book and if you'll phone me at this number we can arrange its return.

You can imagine how relieved I was can't you my address book with all the addresses and phone numbers of all the people I ever call or used to call including you of course though I long since knew your number by heart. And when "Richard" came by on his bike and returned the address book he said it's been driven over more than once pages in it are crushed and folded and they were as if they'd been ironed and it took me some time to straighten them out without tearing them or letting them slip out of the binding because you see even though I'm out-of-touch with a number of people that have moved or are no longer you get the point I can't bring myself to cross them out or paste labels over them and over-write with new names and addresses and telephone numbers because there they are or as we used to tell each other, there it is then, as though that settled matters between us.